Sickness
and Death–
IN THE CHRISTIAN FAMILY

Sickness _and_ Death–
IN THE CHRISTIAN FAMILY

PETER JEFFERY

 EVANGELICAL PRESS

EVANGELICAL PRESS
12 Wooler Street, Darlington, Co. Durham, DL1 1RQ, England

© Evangelical Press 1993
First published 1993

British Library Cataloguing in Publication data available

ISBN 0 85234 308 6

Printed and bound in Great Britain by Cox & Wyman Ltd, Reading

To my mother

Contents

		Page
Introduction		9
1	The family	13
2.	Sending word to Jesus	21
3.	God loves his people	29
4.	The sleep of death	35
5.	Sorrow and comfort	41
6.	The believer's unbelief	49
7.	Jesus wept	55
8.	God is in control	61
9.	The resurrection of the body	67
10.	The Christian under stress	73
11.	Finding rest	81
12.	A personal experience	87

Sickness _and_ Death

IN THE CHRISTIAN FAMILY

Introduction

Some people seem to think that when they become Christians all their troubles will go away. Perhaps they are led to think this way as a result of a certain type of evangelistic preaching which paints the Christian life as a continuous bed of roses. Sooner or later this illusion will be shattered as pain, anguish, sorrow and suffering of all types will touch them. The Bible nowhere promises that the Christian will be immune from these things. On the contrary, the Bible teaches that tribulation and suffering are things the Christian must expect in this world. The night before Calvary, Jesus Christ said, 'In this world you will have trouble. But take heart! I have overcome the world' (John 16:33). Going on to the book of Acts, we find that this is also what the apostles taught. In Acts 14, for instance, we find the apostle Paul going back to the churches he had established on his first missionary journey. He wants to strengthen and encourage them, but he tells them, 'We must go through many hardships to enter the kingdom of God' (v. 22). Trials, problems and sufferings, then, are not to surprise the Christian: rather, the lack of them would be surprising!

Admittedly, the verses we have quoted refer particularly to suffering that arises from persecution and not from sickness; but, whatever the cause of our troubles, the basic principle remains the same. In many ways, suffering that arises from persecution is easier to bear, for at least the Christian can understand its source, and the reason why it occurs. But all too often the Christian who faces sorrow or illness does not know why these things have happened, and this can cause him or her greater spiritual problems.

Some Christians teach that there is no need for believers to endure physical illness. They argue that God has promised to heal all our sicknesses and therefore any unhealed sickness is due to our lack of faith. Our God is Almighty and he can heal, and often does, but not always. Sometimes he says, 'No,' to our prayer for healing and tells us, as he did Paul in 2 Corinthians 12:9, 'My grace is sufficient for you.' Timothy was one of the great instruments God used to establish Christians in the New Testament era, but he was a man with poor health. Paul on occasions was given by God the ability to heal people, but this was not something Paul could do at any time whenever he wanted. Obviously he could not heal Timothy and there is no suggestion in Scripture that Timothy was lacking in faith. Paul's advice to this preacher is: 'Stop drinking only water, and use a little wine because of your stomach and your frequent illnesses' (1 Tim. 5:23). Likewise the apostle left a friend and helper, Trophimus, sick in Miletus (2 Tim. 4:20). Paul himself knew times of illness, but he tells the Galatians that it was because of an illness that he first preached the gospel to them (Gal. 4:13). So, clearly, this illness was no reflection upon the spiritual condition of this great man of faith.

Illness, sickness and death will come to us all; the question is how we as Christians are to face them. Thank God, the Scriptures are full of instructions and encouragements for us. In this book we shall confine ourselves mostly to John 11. Here we have a story of sickness and death in a family that were devoted and earnest Christians. We shall examine their reactions, their feelings, how they coped and how the Lord ministered to them. In the last three chapters we shall move from John 11, firstly to 1 Corinthians 15, to see the reality of the bodily resurrection of all believers, and finally to Psalms 62 and 63 to see how to find rest in God in times of stress.

Sickness _and_ Death
IN THE CHRISTIAN FAMILY

The family

We are introduced in John 11:1 to the family. It consists of a brother and two sisters, Lazarus, Mary and Martha. This was a Christian family, one that loved Jesus. This is brought out clearly in verse 2. It is as if John wants to emphasize the spiritual qualities of these people to whom sorrow and death were soon to come. Matthew, in chapter 26, and Mark, in chapter 14, both mention the incident of the perfume poured upon Jesus, but neither identifies the woman. John does. He wants us to be very clear as to the identity of the Mary to whom he is referring and the uniqueness of her display of love for Jesus. Also, only John mentions that Mary wiped Jesus' feet with her hair.

This family obviously had a deep love for Jesus but, more importantly, Jesus loved them. John declares this plainly in verse 5, and notice also verse 11, where the Saviour acknowledges Lazarus to be 'our friend'.

Lazarus and his sisters lived in the small village of Bethany, a few miles from Jerusalem. It was a village of no real importance, but to Jesus there was a great significance about this small backwater. He saw it, as John tells us in verse 1, as the village of Mary and Martha. When Jesus thought of Bethany he immediately associated it with this family. He thought of their home. It may not have been much by the world's standards, but God's love dwelt there. Robert Murray M'Cheyne expressed it in this way: 'His Father loved that dwelling; for these were justified ones. And angels knew it well; for night and day they ministered there to three heirs of salvation. No wonder he called the place "the town of Mary and her sister Martha". That was its name in heaven... Dear believers, how great the love of Christ is to you! He knows the town where you live — the house where you dwell — the room where you pray. Often he stands at the door — often he puts in his hand at the hole of the door; "I have graven thee on the palms of my hands; thy walls are continually before me." Like a bridegroom loving the place where his bride dwells, so Christ often says, "There they dwell for whom I died." Learn to be like Christ in this. When a merchant looks at a map of the world, his eye turns to those places where his ships are sailing; when a soldier, he looks to the traces of ancient battlefields and fortified towns; but a believer should be like Jesus — he should love the spots where believers dwell.'

John has been very careful in clearly showing us this family. It was one so precious to God, but sickness and death came to it. Lazarus loved Jesus. Jesus loved Lazarus. Yet Lazarus was very sick and was soon to die. There is no contradiction in this. Christians should never doubt the love of God when they are in affliction and should never make the mistake of Job's three friends who concluded that Job must be a wicked man because he suffered so much.

Why do sickness and death come so frequently to those whom God loves? J. C. Ryle answers that perplexing question like this: 'The only explanation that satisfies me is that which the Bible gives. Something has come into the world which has dethroned man from his original position, and stripped him of his original privileges. Something has come in, which, like a handful of gravel thrown into the midst of machinery, has marred the perfect order of God's creation. And what is that something? I answer, in one word, it is sin. "Sin entered into the world, and death by sin" (Rom. 5:12). Sin is the original cause of all the sickness, and disease, and pain, and suffering, which prevail on the earth. They are all part of that curse which came into the world when Adam and Eve ate the forbidden fruit and fell. There would have been no sickness, if there had been no fall. There would have been no sickness, if there had been no sin.'

Ryle is right. Christians live in a world that is plagued by the consequences of sin, but that does not mean that each particular illness is of necessity the result of a particular sin. That is the philosophy of Job's comforters and is clearly wrong. So why does God allow those he has saved from the power and guilt of sin to suffer sickness? The Bible gives three reasons.

1. It is *for our rebuke*. In the famous communion passage in 1 Corinthians 11, Paul refers to sin among Christians that has not been dealt with. He argues that if the church will not deal with it, then God will, and goes on to say in verse 30, 'That is why many among you are weak and sick, and a number of you have fallen asleep [died].' He then declares

why God acts in this way: 'We are being disciplined so that we will not be condemned with the world' (v. 32). In other words, the sickness is a token of God's love for his people and is intended to bring them back into fellowship with him.

While this is a valid biblical reason for some sicknesses, it is not the only reason, or even the main reason.

2. Sickness is also allowed by God *for our blessing*. After Job's comforters have brought their depressing message, a young man by the name of Elihu speaks (Job 32 - 37). This man has a great concept of God: 'How great is God — beyond our understanding!' (Job 36:26). Elihu argues that suffering has a purpose:

'God does all these things to a man...
to turn back his life from the pit,
  that the light of life may shine on him'
(Job 33:29-30).

Before this, Elihu paints a picture of a man with a serious illness (Job 33:19-21). The pain and anguish described here are very real, yet he says in verses 23-26 that this can be a time of rich blessing: 'He sees God's face and shouts for joy.'

It is because of this that Spurgeon was able to say, 'Thank God for good health; thank him even more for bad health.' M'Cheyne shared the same feelings: 'Use afflictions while you have them.' Both these men are saying that there are blessings to be found in sickness that are experienced nowhere else. Sickness can give us more time to meditate and reflect upon the goodness of God that we so often take for granted. Sickness can remind us of how fleeting life is and cause us to value eternity more. Sickness reminds us how weak we are and how dependent upon divine strength and grace. Elihu says in Job 36:15 that God speaks to us in our affliction. May we listen and learn!

3. The third reason, which Jesus tells us in John 11:4 was the reason for Lazarus' illness, is that it is *for God's glory*. How was God glorified in Lazarus' illness? To answer this we need to go back to John 10:24. The Jews said to Jesus, 'How long will you keep us in suspense? If you are the Christ, tell us plainly.' Jesus answered in verse 25 that he was plainly providing proof for them in his miracles, but they would not believe. He then proceeded to do the greatest miracle possible. Lazarus was dead. He was buried and had been in the tomb for four days. His body was beginning to smell as it decayed. Of this there was no doubt and there were many witnesses. Then Jesus, in full view of the crowd, with a word of command, raised Lazarus from the dead. Jesus, by the power of God the Father, conquers death. God was glorified and Jesus declared that he himself is the resurrection and the life. The same is still true. Because Jesus lives we shall live too. The graves will give up their dead. What a blessing that will be for us and what glory for God!

But a word is needed here on how our sicknesses now in this life can glorify God. Turn to 2 Corinthians 12:7-10 and note particularly verses 9-10: 'To keep me from becoming conceited because of these surpassingly great revelations, there was given me a thorn in my flesh, a messenger of Satan, to torment me. Three times I pleaded with the Lord to take it away from me. But he said to me, "My grace is sufficient for you, for my power is made perfect in weakness."

Therefore I will boast all the more gladly about my weaknesses, so that Christ's power may rest on me. That is why, for Christ's sake, I delight in weaknesses, in insults, in hardships, in persecutions, in difficulties. For when I am weak, then I am strong.' God was glorified in the manner in which Paul accepted his affliction and coped with it. No one wants illness and it is our duty to take every proper means to rid ourselves of it. That may mean using medical remedies or spiritual remedies — 'Three times I pleaded with the Lord to take it away from me.' But sometimes neither brings any relief. How do we then, as Christians, react?

J. C. Ryle urges us, 'I exhort all true Christians to remember how much they may glorify God in the time of sickness, and to lie quiet in God's hand when they are ill. I feel it very important to touch on this point. I know how ready the heart of a believer is to faint, and how busy Satan is in suggesting doubts and questionings, when the body of a Christian is weak. I have seen something of the depression and melancholy which sometimes comes upon the children of God when they are suddenly laid aside by disease, and obliged to sit still. I have observed how prone some good people are to torment themselves with morbid thoughts at such seasons, and to say in their hearts, "God has forsaken me: I am cast out of his sight."

'I earnestly entreat all sick believers to remember that they may honour God as much by patient suffering as they can by active work. It often shows more grace to sit still than it does to go to and fro, and perform great exploits. I entreat them to remember that Christ cares for them as much when they are sick as he does when they are well and that every chastisement they feel so acutely is sent in love, and not in anger. Above all, I entreat them to recollect the sympathy of

Jesus for all his weak members. They are always tenderly cared for by him, but never so much as in their time of need. Christ has had great experience of sickness. He knows the heart of a sick man. He used to see "all manner of sickness, and all manner of disease" when he was upon earth. He felt especially for the sick in the days of his flesh. He feels for them specially still. Sickness and suffering, I often think, make believers more like their Lord in experience, than health.'

God can be glorified by the demonstration of his power in delivering us from sickness, but he can also be glorified by the demonstration of his love and grace in the way the Christian copes with his or her suffering. We may argue that it is not easy. Far from being easy, it is impossible in our own strength. God promises, 'My grace is sufficient for you.' Note that it is grace, not will-power, nor strength of character, nor stoic endurance that we need.

When illness comes, there are two possible questions to ask: 'Why?' or 'How?' '*Why* does God allow me to suffer like this?' To ask why only compounds the problem. It insinuates that something of merit is involved and I do not deserve this. Also it includes more than a little self-pity. '*How* can I use this illness to glorify God? *How* in this difficult time can I learn more of God? *How* can my illness help others?' If we live in this attitude, Christians and non-Christians will observe it and will appreciate something of the love and mercy of God. God is thus glorified.

We shall conclude this chapter with another quotation from J. C. Ryle: 'The day may come when, after a long fight with disease, we shall feel that medicine can do no more, and that nothing remains but to die. Friends will be standing by, unable to help us. Hearing, eyesight, even the power of praying, will be fast failing us. The world and its shadows will be melting beneath our feet. Eternity, with its realities, will be looming large before our minds. What shall support us in that trying hour? What shall enable us to feel, "I will fear no evil"? (Ps. 23:4). Nothing, nothing can do it but close communion with Christ. Christ dwelling in our hearts by faith, Christ putting his right arm under our heads, Christ felt to be sitting by our side, Christ can alone give us the victory in the last struggle.

'Let us cleave to Christ more closely, love him more heartily, live to him more thoroughly, copy him more exactly, confess him more boldly, follow him more fully. Religion like this will always bring its own reward. Worldly people may laugh at it. Weak brethren may think it extreme. But it will wear well. In sickness it will bring us peace. In the world to come it will give us a crown of glory that fades not away.'

Sickness *and* Death
IN THE CHRISTIAN FAMILY

Chapter 2

Sending word to Jesus

When Lazarus was taken ill his sisters were understandably very concerned. We are not told so in Scripture, but the probability is that they obtained for him any medical help that was available. What we are told in John 11:3 is that they sent word to Jesus. This is the natural response of all those who love the Lord, because they want Jesus to be involved in their problems. The relationship between the Christian and the Lord Jesus Christ is not a formal or official one; it is one of deep love and passion. This is revealed clearly here in verses 2, 3, 5 and 11. Therefore the Christian knows the Saviour is concerned and cares not only for our souls, but for our bodies as well. Jesus demonstrated this concern of God in a most amazing statement when he said that God had numbered every hair on our heads. So without hesitation Mary and Martha sent word to Jesus.

We know that Jesus is omniscient and that he knows

everything. It was this great truth that so affected and convinced Nathaniel that Jesus was the Christ (John 1:45-51). So Jesus has no *need* to be told anything, but he *wants* to be told. He wants to see our love for him demonstrated in our sending word to him.

In Psalm 50:15 God instructs us to call upon him in the day of trouble. This calling upon God is not for the purpose of passing on facts of which he is unaware, but to show our love and dependence. In John 20 Jesus asked the tearful Mary Magdalene, 'Why are you crying?' This was not a rebuke, neither was it asked because he did not know the reason for the tears. He wanted her to unburden her heart before him. 'Cast your burden upon the Lord,' is the encouragement of Scripture and this is what Mary and Martha were doing.

In his book *If God already knows, why pray?* Douglas Kelly makes the following point: 'The sovereign God on his throne, who has planned all things from the beginning to the end, has arranged His plan in such a way that the prayers of the saints are one of the major means He uses to accomplish His final goal. Instead of the sovereignty of God clashing with the prayers of the believer, the two actually presuppose one another and fulfil and undergird one another. God made His world and ordered His plan in such a way that when we become burdened and concerned over some situation, He uses it for good, even to further His purposes. In fact, He lays the burden on us. For example we find ourselves under pressure, in a predicament that we cannot resolve, and so we begin to pray.'

Charles Spurgeon put it this way: 'It is well said that asking is the rule of the kingdom. It is a rule that will never be altered in anybody's case. If the royal and divine Son of

God cannot be exempted from the rule of asking that He may have, you and I cannot expect to have the rule relaxed in our favour. God will bless Elijah and send rain on Israel, but Elijah must pray for it. If the chosen nation is to prosper, Samuel must plead for it. If the Jews are to be delivered, Daniel must intercede. God will bless Paul, and the nations shall be converted through him, but Paul must pray. Pray he did, without ceasing; his epistles show that he expected nothing except by asking for it.'

For us, sending word to Jesus means prayer and this is a crucial part of the Christian life. We can only pray because God loves us and is therefore willing to hear our cries, but we must also pray because we love him and want him involved in our trials and problems. Of course, prayer is much more than casting our burdens upon the Lord, but we are thinking of it now in the context of sickness and sorrow. God cares because God loves us, and what a delight this is to a troubled soul! Irrespective of the answer, merely to pray is a comfort. If we are only comforted when God says, 'Yes,' to our prayers, it means our comfort is not in God himself, but only in the benefits he hands out. That is a very shallow love. God *himself* is our strength. This means that in times of distress, strength is not something God hands out like some divine aspirin. Strength comes from communion and oneness with God, and prayer brings us into that oneness. So prayer does not so much change *things* as change *us*. True prayer, that is not dictating to God or demanding of God, but pours out the deep feelings of our hearts in requests and petitions, will bring our minds into tune with the Old Testament saint who said, 'Though he slay me, yet will I hope in him' (Job 13:15).

Prevailing prayer

As A. W. Pink tells us, 'The sisters of Lazarus acquainted the Lord with the desperate condition of their brother, appealed to His love and then left the case in His hands, to be dealt with as He saw best. They were not so irreverent as to tell Him what to do. In this they have left all praying souls a worthy example which we do well to follow. "Commit thy way unto the Lord": that is our responsibility. "Trust also in him": that is our privilege. Trust also in Him, not dictate to Him, and not demand from Him. People talk of "claiming" from God. But grace cannot be claimed, and all is of grace. The very throne we approach is one of grace. How utterly incongruous then to talk of claiming anything from the Sitter on such a throne. "Commit thy way unto the Lord, trust also in him, and he shall bring it to pass." But it must ever be kept in mind that He will bring it to pass in His own sovereign way and in His own appointed time. And often-times, usually so in fact, His way and time will be different from ours. He brought it to pass for Martha and Mary, though not in the time and way they probably expected.'

The sisters' message to Jesus was simply: 'Lord, the one you love is sick.' It was simple but most illuminating. The word 'Lord' shows the relationship between Christ and the Christian. It is based on love, but it is not a relationship of equals. It acknowledges Jesus as their Master and them-selves as disciples. There is warmth, passion and feeling in the message, but not at the expense of reverence.

Next we see one of the great secrets of prevailing prayer. If an unbeliever had been sending the message to Jesus he would have argued, 'Jesus, the one who loves you is sick — the one who has done so many things for you, sacrificed for you, suffered for you. Come on, Jesus, he deserves your help! He has earned it.' Not so Mary and Martha. Their hope rests not on Lazarus' love for Jesus, but on Jesus' love for Lazarus. His love, not ours, is the great strength of prevailing prayer. Jesus loved Lazarus with an everlasting love before creation, with a sustaining love that kept him day by day. This is our blessed hope and joy. This is the way to plead with Jesus.

James says, 'You ask and do not receive, because you ask in the wrong way.' We ask proudly, making demands as if we were special people, so that if Christ were to grant our request he would be feeding our pride. Robert Murray M'Cheyne said, 'Learn to lie in the dust and plead His free love.' They did not pray, 'Lord, come and heal our brother.' They merely left the problem in the divine hands. We find this most difficult, but M'Cheyne reminds us 'that urgency in prayer does not so much consist in vehement pleading, as in vehement believing. He that believes most the love and power of Jesus, will obtain most in prayer.' It is true that the Bible gives examples of strong pleadings and it certainly does not forbid them, but there is what M'Cheyne calls 'a holy delicacy in prayer'.

Mary and Martha had such a sweet and blessed trust in Jesus that all they needed to say was, 'Lord, the one you love is sick.' The power of prayer is not its length or passion, but the fact that God cares.

The answer

If we assume that the words of Jesus in verse 4, 'This sickness will not end in death,' were addressed to the one who had brought Mary and Martha's message, and it was intended for the sisters, then it was certainly an answer to kindle hope. It is not difficult to imagine these women waiting for Jesus' answer. Lazarus was getting weaker and weaker; then the answer came. Their relief must have been immense and no doubt they told Lazarus. But still he grew weaker and death seemed very near. But Jesus said, this sickness will not end in death, so they still went on hoping. Then Lazarus died, and so did their hope. The words of Jesus must have seemed a mockery to them. As they carried their brother to the grave, their faith was buried with him. Jesus had said he would not die, but he was dead!

Sickness and the death of a loved one can put a Christian's faith under severe stress. Was Mary's refusal in verse 20 to come to meet Jesus the result of this? Even if we are doing Mary an injustice by suggesting this, and verse 20 is simply in line with her reserved temperament, as most of the commentators suggest, it is sadly true that the death of a loved one has had a severe effect upon the faith of many Christians. One reason for this is that we sometimes misinterpret the words and promises of Scripture. Take Mary and Martha, for instance. How did they interpret the words of Jesus when he said, 'This sickness will not end in death'? In their anxiety to see their brother well, they obviously believed the words meant he would not die. Indeed, there seemed to be no other logical or sensible way of understanding the answer. But there was another way. It was impossible to the logic or reason of men and women, but the fact was that the illness did not end in death but in resurrection.

When a loved one is seriously ill and we pray for healing we may come to believe from a particular verse or circumstance that God has heard our prayer and promised to heal the sick person. This thrills us and we share it with great joy with other believers. What happens then if the loved one dies? Do we blame God and accuse him of breaking his promises? Or do we acknowledge that there was no promise — only our strong subjective feelings telling us what we wanted to hear. Christians need to be extremely careful in such situations that we correctly interpret what God is saying and we need to learn to distinguish between our subjective feelings and the truth of God.

I remember a very fine Christian, a man not given to making rash statements, who was convinced that the Lord had promised that he would live to see his grandchildren. So convinced was he that he told his family. You can imagine the confusion in his sons' minds when their father died suddenly when they were teenagers. Understandably their first thought was, 'Why did God break his promise to Dad?' Of course, God had not broken his promise. Dad was mistaken, but it was a mistake that caused more grief than was necessary.

Thank God that he does make promises, and on occasion he does heal the sick. He is infallible, but we are not. We need to trust him totally in whatever circumstances may come our way. Ultimately, like Mary and Martha, our tears will give way to joy and our confusion to understanding and praise.

Sickness *and* Death—
IN THE CHRISTIAN FAMILY

Chapter 3

God loves his people

John 11: 5 tells us that Jesus loved Martha and her sister and Lazarus. This whole family was engulfed in the love of God and in times of sorrow and distress there is no greater comfort to the Christian than to know this. It was certainly a source of great strength and hope to Mary and Martha during their brother's illness. Because of God's love they knew they could turn to Jesus and expect help. True, the help did not come in the way they expected, but it did come. Their hope and plea for Lazarus was that Jesus loved him.

This is so important that it is not surprising that the devil seeks to destroy the awareness of God's love in the Christian's heart. When you yourself are ill, or someone you love is ill, it is easy to grow bitter and critical and therefore lose sight of God's love. That is the work of Satan. Or perhaps we still talk theoretically about the divine love, but we have ceased to know and feel it. That too is Satan's work.

So we need to ask the question, 'How do we know that God loves us?' The answer must be more than just subjective feelings. These are important, but all too often they are the first things the devil attacks during a period of prolonged illness. At such times our feelings become vulnerable and it is not enough therefore to say, 'I know God loves me because I feel it in my heart.' What about the times when you do *not* feel it? A prolonged illness can make us feel forgotten, sorry for ourselves, depressed and lonely. This is particularly true if we cannot get to church and we miss out on ministry and fellowship. At such times our love for God may wane and we need then the great objective truth of the gospel to keep us aware of God's love. Listen to Jeremiah 31:3: 'I have loved you with an everlasting love: I have drawn you with loving-kindness.'

The proof that God loves us is revealed in the actions of God in salvation. As Jeremiah 31:3 says, he draws us to himself. The same truth is demonstrated in John 3:16. When God so loved the world it was not an empty emotional gesture, but issued forth in a particular act of salvation — he gave his one and only Son to die on the cross to save us. The proof that God loves us is that he has saved us. M'Cheyne puts it like this: 'When the Lord Jesus draws near to a dead, carnal sinner, and reveals to him a glimpse of his own beauty — of his face fairer than the sons of men — of his precious blood — of the room that there is under his wings; and when the soul is drawn away from its deadness, darkness, and worldliness, and is persuaded to forsake all, and flow toward the Lord Jesus — then that soul is made to taste the peace of believing, and is made to know that Jesus loves him.'

The great objective truths of the gospel, the incarnation of God, the cross, the shed blood, grace and mercy, need to be in our minds continually and particularly during times of sorrow and distress. These evidences of the love of God are like great immovable rocks amidst a sea of changing circumstances. The trouble with many Christians is that they feel too much and think too little, and it is these believers who have the most trouble coping with illness and death. Have you noticed that the same Christians who can know heights of great spiritual joy can also know depths of utter despair? The reason is that the feelings which lift them and so enrich their spiritual lives can also, if left unchecked, sink them and impoverish their spiritual lives. So for a healthy, balanced Christian life we need both subjective feelings and objective truth. Feel and think, and then in times of sorrow you will not lose sight of God's love.

Different individuals

It is good to be reminded that Jesus loved all three individuals that made up this particular family in Bethany. We know little of the character of Lazarus, but Mary and Martha were so different from each other. It seems from Luke 10:38-42 that Mary was the more spiritual of the sisters. But in John 11 Martha stands out as the more stable character. In verse 20 she comes running to Jesus while Mary stays at home, and while both sisters say, 'Lord, if you had been here, my brother would not have died,' only Martha adds, 'But I know that even now God will give you whatever you ask.' We shall deal with these statements later, but for now they reveal how different was the temperament and character of the sisters. Yet Jesus loved them both.

Temperamentally reliable or unstable, spiritually weak

or strong, Jesus loves all his people. What a comfort this is to us, and it has real implications in experience. We may see a Christian family go through all sorts of distress and sorrow, and in it all they know the love and peace of God in a most comforting way. Then we have to face the same thing. Will we know the same comforting presence of Jesus? We may feel they are more spiritual people than we are, a closer family, stronger characters and therefore we cannot expect to cope as they did. But we can, because Jesus loves us. He loves all his people. We need to believe that and hold on to it. God does not love you any less than he loved Mary and Martha and Lazarus. Weak or strong, if we are Christians he loves us with a love that knows no degree and no fluctuation, but continues as a steady, glorious, divine love for us in joy or sorrow.

If in your trials you do not know the love and peace of God, it is because you are relying too much on feelings — so you need to think more. Or it may be because your doctrine is wrong and you believe that Christians should never be ill, or that God will always heal them. If you became ill and God did not heal you, you could then believe it was because your faith was not strong enough, and you would feel guilty and feel far away from God's love and peace.

Love delays

Having read in verse 5 that Jesus loved this family, we might expect to see him then rushing to their aid. If someone you loved was seriously ill, you would probably drop everything and dash to be with them, yet Jesus did not. It is clear from verse 6 that the delay was deliberate and two reasons are given. The first is in verse 4: the sickness was for God's glory, that Jesus should be glorified through the miracle that was to follow; the second is in verse 15, and is that the believers should be strengthened in their faith.

The translation of verse 6 in the NIV is not very helpful. It seems to indicate a contradiction between Jesus' love for this family and his action. D. A. Carson writes, 'The NIV's rendering of the opening of v. 6 is without linguistic defence: "Yet when he heard…" The translators have set the affirmation of Jesus' love (v. 5) in dramatic tension with the two-day delay reported in v. 6.' In fact, as Carson goes on to point out, the two-day delay was motivated by the Saviour's love for Mary, Martha and Lazarus. There is no doubt that the delay caused great grief to the family and Jesus could have prevented that. This does not contradict his love for them, but rather highlights his love for God the Father and the whole of God's people, as the reasons in verses 4 and 15 reveal. Inevitably, we tend to see our pain and suffering simply as they affect us personally, and fail to realize that these things also have an effect upon the glory of God and other people around us. We forget this, but God never does, and hence the wisdom of the words of J. C. Ryle: 'The pain of the few was permitted for the benefit of the whole church of Christ.'

Carson explains further: 'The delay ensured that Lazarus had been dead long enough that no one could misinterpret the miracle as a mere resuscitation, effected before the man's spirit had properly left the area. The miracle that Jesus actually performed therefore confirmed the faith of his disciples and friends with dramatic power that would have been lacking if Jesus had responded immediately to the plea for help.'

If at times God appears to be slow in coming to our aid, it is not because he does not care, but it may be that he has other purposes to fulfil through our pain. We must learn not merely to accept this, but be willing to be used by God. The Lord's providential ways often seem to us to be baffling, but the end purpose is always to our benefit. Mary, Martha and Lazarus had pain and anguish, but what blessing for us to be able to read this story!

Judge not the Lord by feeble sense,
But trust him for his grace;
Behind a frowning providence
He hides a smiling face.

His purposes will ripen fast,
Unfolding every hour;
The bud may have a bitter taste,
But sweet will be the flower.

(William Cowper).

Sickness _and_ Death

IN THE CHRISTIAN FAMILY

Chapter 4

The sleep of death

John 11:11-13 brings before us a very refreshing and comforting concept of the death of a Christian. Jesus said that Lazarus had fallen asleep. Very clearly from verse 14, he meant that Lazarus was dead. The apostles misunderstood what the Lord was saying and thought Jesus meant natural sleep, so they reasoned that sleep would do their sick friend good. We can see two probable reasons for the misunderstanding. Firstly, they had been told that the sickness would not end in death, and secondly, if Lazarus was asleep and there was the probability that he would get better, then there was no need for them to go to Judea, and it is evident from verse 8 that they were reluctant to go to Bethany.

The question arises, why did Jesus not say plainly in the first place that Lazarus was dead? Why did he speak of sleep when he meant death? J. C. Ryle's answer is that sleep 'is a gentle and pathetic way of expressing the most painful of events that can befall man, and a most suitable one, when we remember that after death comes resurrection. In dying we are not annihilated. Like sleepers we lie down, to rise again.' This concept of the death of God's people is common throughout Scripture.

'Give light to my eyes, or I will sleep in death' (Ps. 13:3).

'When he had said this, he fell asleep. And Saul was there giving approval to his death' (Acts 7:60).

'Then those also who have fallen asleep in Christ are lost. If only for this life we have hope in Christ, we are to be pitied more than all men' (1 Cor. 15:18).

'Brothers, we do not want you to be ignorant about those who fall asleep, or to grieve like the rest of men, who have no hope. We believe that Jesus died and rose again and so we believe that God will bring with Jesus those who have fallen asleep in him' (1 Thess. 4:13-14).

So the death of believers is often compared to sleep. But we need at this point to sound a word of caution. Sleep is only applied to the death of *believers* — never to the death of unbelievers. Also we need to note that the biblical use of the word 'sleep' is not the same as the Jehovah's Witnesses' doctrine of soul sleep, which virtually means soul annihilation and is the basis of their rejection of the reality of hell. Loraine Boettner makes the point that 'Everyone acknowledges, of course, that the body does sleep until the resurrection, that is, it becomes unconscious, insensible. The sleep spoken of is that of the body, not of the soul. Those who teach soul sleep have simply confused the sleep of the body with that of the soul. Soul sleep is not taught anywhere in the Bible. In every instance in which the word sleep is used in connection with the dead, the context makes it clear that it applies only to the body.'

The death of a Christian

The word 'sleep' is used to show us that death for a Christian is no terrible experience to be dreaded and feared. Here are some of the ways Matthew Henry has described it: 'A good Christian when he dies does but sleep: he rests from the labours of the day past, and is refreshing himself for the next morning.' 'The grave to the wicked is a prison, and its grave-clothes as the shackles of a criminal reserved for execution, but to the godly death is a bed and all its bands as the soft and downy fetters of an easy quiet sleep.' 'Though the body is corrupt, it will rise in the morning as if it had never seen corruption: it is but putting off your clothes to be mended and trimmed up for the marriage day, the coronation day, to which we must rise.'

These thoughts of Matthew Henry are completely in line with the way the Bible speaks of the death of a child of God.

It is precious in the sight of the Lord (Ps. 116:15).
It is to go to paradise at once (Luke 23:43).
It is to go to the Father's house (John 14:2).
It is to be with Christ (Phil. 1:23).
It is to be at home with the Lord (2 Cor. 5:8).
It is gain (Phil. 1:21).
It is far better (Phil. 1:23).

This is the way Christians are to regard death, and what a blessing it then becomes! John Wesley could say of the first Methodists, 'Our people die well.' This was true because they believed what the Scriptures said about death. Richard Baxter, the Puritan, was asked on his deathbed: 'How are you?' His answer was: 'Almost well and almost home.' Another Puritan, Richard Sibbes, said, 'Death is only a grim porter to let us into a stately palace.' The nineteenth-century American evangelist, D. L. Moody, said on his deathbed: 'Earth recedes. Heaven opens before me. If this is death, it is sweet. There is no dark valley here. God is calling me and I must go. This is my triumph. This is my Coronation Day.' Iain Murray, in his biography of Dr Martyn Lloyd-Jones, writes, 'Among his last audible words were those spoken to his consultant, Grant Williams, who visited him on February 24th. Mr Williams wanted to give him antibiotics. ML-J shook his head in disagreement. "Well," said his doctor, "when the Lord's time comes, even though I fill you up to the top of your head with antibiotics, it won't make any difference." His patient shook his head. "I want to make you comfortable, more comfortable," Williams went on, "it grieves me to see you sitting here 'weary and worn and sad'" (quoting from Bonar's well-known hymn). That was too much for ML-J. "Not sad!" he declared. "Not sad!" The truth was that he believed the work of dying was done and he was ready to go.'

Facing death

Dying may be a problem for the Christian, with the pain and anguish that may be involved, but death itself should pose no problem. People without Christ are terrified by death, and quite rightly so, because after death there is the judgement. Vavasor Powell, the Welsh Puritan, said, 'The fear of death is ingrafted in the common nature of all men, but faith works it out of Christians.' This should be the experience of all Christians, but sadly it is not always true, and we allow the world's attitude towards death to affect us. It is not unusual that when a Christian is dying the family takes every precaution to keep the truth from him. Why is this? Is death for us so final and awful? If the family is not Christian and the person who is dying is not a Christian, then we can understand this attitude and the reasoning behind it. One may even go so far as to say that on a rare occasion, in certain circumstances, it may be wise to withhold the truth from a Christian, but surely not generally. Such a position makes it impossible to minister to the dying saint because everyone is acting a part and the truth is being suppressed.

What a Christian needs above all when he is dying is to know the love and peace of God. To have the things of God ministered to him is his right and privilege. To be reminded that death has lost its sting and the grave its victory; to be shown again the victory of Christ on his behalf is better than any medication. 'Our God is the end of the journey,' is a truth not only to be sung in one of our great hymns, but also to be rejoiced in when the end is drawing near.

What happens when a Christian dies?

The spirit, saved and washed in the blood of Jesus, goes immediately to heaven. Jesus said, 'Today you will be with me in Paradise,' and that is why Paul could say with every confidence that to die is gain. In 2 Corinthians 5:8, the apostle tells us that to be away from the body is to be at home with the Lord.

The body goes to the grave, to decay and corruption, to

await the coming of the Lord and the resurrection. The promise of Jesus is that he will raise us up on the last day (see John 6:39,40,44,54; 1 Cor. 15:42-44,51-57). At the resurrection the body and spirit will be united to be for ever with the Lord.

All this means that for the Christian death is not some terrifying unknown. We know more about what will happen to us when we die than we do about what will happen to us next year. The Bible says we shall be with the Lord and we shall be like him. We shall awake to a new day. To quote Matthew Henry again, it will be like putting our clothes off to be mended and pressed ready for the great coronation day.

Sickness *and* Death

IN THE CHRISTIAN FAMILY

Sorrow and comfort

We are taken in John 11:17-20 into this Christian home at Bethany in the days immediately following the death of Lazarus, and we see that it is a home full of sorrow and weeping. This does not mean that Mary and Martha were unspiritual and lacked faith. Confidence and faith in Christ's triumph over death and the grave do not turn us into unfeeling robots. When Paul tells us in 1 Thessalonians 4:13 that we are not to grieve like the rest of men who have no hope, he is not telling us not to grieve at all. Tears are not out of place at a Christian's funeral, but they are not the tears of hopelessness. If we believe all that we saw in the previous chapter, then we cannot grieve for the departed loved one. We have no fears for the one who has died and we do not need to pray for him or her. What could you pray for someone who is already in the presence of our God and Saviour? Our tears are for our own sad loss. We loved this person and we shall miss him. Our sorrow is a normal reflection of our love and mingled with it is the joy that our loved one has gone to the heavenly home.

Loraine Boettner uses the following illustration: 'Suppose a relative or friend is given a trip around the world with all expenses paid, all hotel accommodations and sightseeing tours arranged, and in association with a very desirable group of friends. Suppose the trip includes a tour of our Rocky Mountain and Pacific coast states, a luxury liner or airplane across the Pacific to Hawaii, Japan, Australia, India, Egypt, Palestine, Greece, Italy, Switzerland, Germany, France, England, and back across the Atlantic. Such a trip would be considered a great privilege. It would mean temporary separation, but we would be happy that our friend should have such a privilege, and we would look forward to seeing him after the trip was over. The experience of death is somewhat like that — the breaking of personal ties, temporary separation, then permanent reunion in that better land. Even in this world when friends come together after years of separation, the intervening time seems to fade away as if there had been no separation at all.'

Tears of sorrow are not the same as the wailing of despair, but if that sorrow continues over a length of time it can degenerate into an unbelieving despair. But in those early days after a death it is normal and healthy. The sad loss will be felt for years but the sorrow and grief turn for strength to the goodness and love of God. What a person believes will unquestionably affect how he or she copes with death. Boettner says, 'The only way for a Christian to meet sorrow is to meet it as his Master did, calmly and courageously, with implicit faith that whatever our Father in heaven does is right—"Not my will, but thine be done." The glorious thing about this is that even the weakest and most ignorant among us can have this faith if he will but keep open the channel of communication between himself and his heavenly Father.'

We need also to remember that different circumstances of death produce different intensities of sorrow. For instance, if an old saint, perhaps someone in his eighties, who is just longing to go home to heaven, dies, then the sorrow will not be quite the same as if a young child or someone in the prime of life is taken. But thank God that in every circumstance of death the Christian's tears are softened by faith in the one who said, 'I am the resurrection and the life. He who believes in me will live, even though he dies.'

The comfort of friends

We are told in John 11:19 that many friends came to comfort Mary and Martha in their sad loss. These were not Christian friends but Jews from nearby Jerusalem. In times of sorrow a visit from friends and family can be greatly appreciated by the bereaved, but a Christian especially appreciates the comfort that comes from other believers. Paul urges us in Romans 12:13-15 to 'share with God's people who are in need…' and to 'mourn with those who mourn'. The comfort that a Christian can give to another Christian is quite unique. Others can show concern and kindness, and that is needed and appreciated, but only a Christian can encourage and minister to the sorrowing one.

The passage in 1 Thessalonians 4:13-18 ends with the words: 'Therefore encourage each other with these words,' and the words referred to are these: 'According to the Lord's own word, we tell you that we who are still alive, who are left till the coming of the Lord, will certainly not precede those who have fallen asleep. For the Lord himself will come down from heaven, with a loud command, with the voice of the archangel and with the trumpet call of God, and the dead in Christ will rise first. After that, we who are still alive and are left will be caught up with them in the clouds to meet the Lord in the air. And so we will be with the Lord for ever.'

Clearly what the apostle has in mind is far more than just a social visit, so let us not be slow in this ministry when the need arises. A visit, a phone call or a letter can be greatly used by God to comfort a soul in sorrow.

A Christian man's testimony at the time of the tragic death of his two children was: 'The next few days we were greatly encouraged by the fellowship of Christian friends. They comforted us in our distress and prayed with us in our time of need, and we felt the power of their prayers in that difficult period. After the funeral I was relieved when the many family members and friends who were not Christians had gone home. I love them, but their words were so empty and their grief without hope. That may sound a little uncharitable, but we both felt that the Lord's people were closer to us and we looked forward to seeing them first of all.'

It is possible in times of deep sorrow to lose our spiritual bearings and God will use other Christians to remind us of the sort of truths that are mentioned in 1 Thessalonians 4. We comfort each other with the truth of the gospel and also with our own experience of God's goodness when we were in trouble. God 'comforts us in all our troubles, so that we can comfort those in any trouble with the comfort we ourselves have received from God' (2 Cor. 1:4).

The God of all comfort

2 Corinthians 4:5 speaks of comfort overflowing. What a
marvellous description this is of the ministry of the Lord
Jesus Christ to his people in their need! Mary and Martha no
doubt appreciated the comfort of their friends, but comfort
only began to overflow when Jesus came to them. But such
was the depth of their sorrow and the added pain caused by
their misunderstanding of the words of Jesus that this
comfort did not come easily.

We have already seen in Luke 10:38-42 that Mary was
probably the more spiritual of the two sisters, but when
Jesus came to Bethany it was Martha who rushed out to meet
him while Mary sat at home. Sometimes the more spiritually
sensitive believer finds it more difficult to deal with sickness and death than the more robust, practical Christian.
This is because such people feel deeply. The same passion-
ate feelings that could cause Mary to pour expensive perfume on Jesus and wipe his feet with her hair now cause her
to sit sad and dejected at home instead of rushing to meet the
Saviour. Feelings and emotion are God-given, but they must
not be allowed to rule our lives. They must always be
subservient to the Word of God. The word of God to the
sisters in verse 4 was: 'This sickness will not end in death.'
Both believed in the ability of Jesus to fulfil that promise and
both say, 'If you had been here, my brother would not have
died.' Mary makes the statement and then weeps at the
apparent failure of Jesus. Martha voices the same words but
adds, 'But I know that even now God will give you whatever
you ask.' The difference was between despair and hope.

Having said that, it is clear that Martha's hope was mixed
with all sorts of confusion and doubt. What did she mean
when she said, 'But even now...'? (v. 22). She could only

have had one thing in mind. There was only one thing that could help the dead Lazarus, and it was not healing but life. Yet she never actually asks for this, and when Jesus virtually promises it — 'Your brother will rise again' (v. 23) — she backpedals (v. 24). She moves from life now to resurrection at the last day. William Hendriksen comments: 'In the heart of Martha the darkness of grief and the light of hope were engaged in deadly combat. Sometimes her lips gave expression to her near-despair; then again to her optimism. Here is a woman, deeply emotional. But, here is also a disciple of Jesus, her soul filled with reverence for her Lord. Here is, consequently, a heart, stirred to its depths, and swaying between grief and hope.'

Do not we all know something of swaying between grief and hope? Sometimes, when a loved one is very ill, we long for God to heal and ask in prayer for this, but at the same time we are not really sure if we believe it is possible. Or, on the other hand, we demand healing. We tell God he must heal and then convince ourselves he will, but the conviction is based on no more than desperate longings. Swaying between grief and hope can cause much confusion, so we must learn to guard ourselves against unbelief and also against the presumption of trusting a word God has never spoken.

Our great comfort at such times is the character and being of the God of all comfort. There is always sympathy from heaven for our earthly sorrows. Isaiah 63:9 tells us, 'In all their distresses he too was distressed.' Jesus draws near to us, as he did to Mary and Martha, and thank God that the sympathy of heaven is not helpless pity but a working power that meets our need. God may not choose to heal or raise the dead, but he will always comfort his people with tokens of divine love and peace, and with an awareness of his presence. This we can and ought to know.

So in our sorrows we look first not for the power of God to deliver, but for the presence of God to comfort. It is possible to be satisfied with God's presence and not need to look for his power to heal. On his deathbed Dr Lloyd-Jones wrote on a scrap of paper for his family, 'Do not pray for healing. Do not hold me back from glory.' There are three words to remember: presence, peace, power. It is only when we are aware of God's presence and peace that we can ask for his power. If God gives it, then praise his name. If not, then still praise his name because you continue to have his presence and peace and when these are real there will be no bitterness, no accusations and no losing of faith.

Sickness *and* Death

IN THE CHRISTIAN FAMILY

The believer's unbelief

From John 11:24 it is clear that Martha believed in the resurrection of the dead, but it is also clear that this brought her no comfort in her present sorrow. She is in effect saying, 'I know my brother has gone to heaven and I believe the body we have buried will rise again on the last day, but what good is that to me now?' Most of us are like this, but it should not be so. We allow our present sorrows to make a deeper impression on us than our belief in future glory. We are, if we are honest, unable to say with Paul, 'I consider that our present sufferings are not worth comparing with the glory that will be revealed in us' (Rom. 8:18). It is the basic problem of not living by faith but by sight.

Martha says she believes a great truth, yet there is an evident tone of disappointment in her speech. It was too far away; she wanted it now. Whilst we can all identify ourselves with this attitude, we must never condone it. It calls into serious question the depth and reality of our faith in Christ. Many Christians complain that they do not feel an inward peace and comfort. Very often the reason is that they have vague and indefinite views of God. What they say they believe, they have never properly thought through. Consequently the truths that ought to comfort them do not, and the reason is not the truth but the Christian's lack of understanding. Ryle said, 'We are many of us sadly like Martha. A little general knowledge of Christ as the only Saviour is often all we possess. But of the fulness that dwells in him, of his resurrection, priesthood, intercession and unfailing compassion, we have tasted little or nothing at all.'

It is not unusual today to hear Christians complain of the lack of application in the sermons they hear. This may be fair comment. A preacher who fails to apply the Scriptures to the present needs of his congregation is failing miserably. Preaching is more than teaching facts. But while accepting this, it must be said that we cannot apply what we do not know. Teaching and Bible knowledge are essential for every Christian, otherwise preaching would only be supplying painkillers to deal with a single present problem and not also giving great biblical principles that enable the hearers to cope with every situation. There is a great danger that we are producing a generation of spoon-fed Christians who cannot think for themselves and need everything spelt out for them. This produces endless backslidings and insecure believers. J. C. Ryle puts his finger on the point when he asks, 'What right have we to wonder that we feel so little comfort in our Christianity? Our slight and imperfect knowledge of Christ is the true reason for our discomfort. The root of happy religion is clear, distinct, well-defined knowledge of Jesus Christ. More knowledge would have saved Martha many sighs and tears.'

Of course, knowledge alone is not enough, but without it our faith will be impoverished and impotent.

Resurrection

For the Christian, knowledge is not just an awareness of facts. It also involves a fellowship and union with Christ. So the great words of Jesus in verse 25, 'I am the resurrection and the life,' are more than just a statement of thrilling truths; they are also an invitation to find comfort in Jesus himself. The comfort Martha needs will be found in Jesus, who has conquered death and can give and sustain life.

Resurrection means that death is not the end. It means a return to life, and Jesus alone is the conveyer of this, because he is the source and fountain of all life. At the beginning of John's Gospel we read that 'In him [Jesus] was life, and that life was the light of men' (John 1:4). That this was no idle boast was soon to be evidenced in the cemetery at Bethany, and even more so in the Saviour's own resurrection. There is no life apart from Jesus. All that men know outside of Christ is death. We are born in a condition of spiritual death. Physical death will therefore usher us into eternal death. Only Jesus can change this, because he alone is the resurrection and the life.

The effects of what Jesus is are enormous for his people. But when he said, 'He who believes in me,' he is limiting what he is going to say. The promise is not true for everyone, only for believers. He promises two things. Firstly, the Christian who dies will live. This means that death cannot change the blessed gift of life that Jesus has given his people. Lazarus has died and this inevitably changes his relationship with his family, but not with his God and

Saviour. Physical death does not affect spiritual life and this is true of all believers. The second promise is that whoever lives and believes in Christ, whoever has the gift of spiritual life, will never die eternally. Heaven is the abode of all those who die in Christ.

When we stand at the graveside of a believer, what a comfort these truths are! Sure and certain hope of resurrection unto life eternal is not an empty platitude, but the promise of God for all who believe in Christ.

Do you believe this?

Having made the statement, Jesus then challenges Martha and all Christians, 'Do you believe this?' How we answer the challenge will decide how we cope with death, because the challenge is also the comfort. So often we look for comfort in our feelings and Jesus says, 'Comfort is in your faith, in what you believe.'

If we really believe this it removes the fear of death. It must do so because if to live is Christ, then to die is gain. Outside of Christ, to live is sin. This is the teaching of Romans chapters 5 and 6. Sin is the dominant feature in every life, and therefore death reigns. Salvation deals with sin. On the cross Jesus paid the debt our sin incurred and we died to sin and its dominance. Christ now has become the dominant one in our lives. This does not mean that the Christian is sinless, but it does mean that the final and ultimate victory over sin and death is assured. Death must therefore be gain for us because we shall then know an eternity of pure and perfect fellowship with Jesus. For our loved ones who die in Christ, it gives us a blessed hope and joy. We mourn for our loss, but rejoice in their gain. They have gone home to glory. Do we believe this? If we do, then we can rejoice with the hymnist:

> For yonder a light shines eternal,
> Which spreads through the valley of gloom;
> Lord Jesus, resplendent and regal,
> Drives fear far away from the tomb.
> Our God is the end of the journey,
> His pleasant and glorious domain;
> For there are the children of mercy,
> Who praise him for Calvary's pain.

(Vernon Higham).

Jesus wept

'Jesus wept' (John 11:35) is well known as the shortest verse in the Bible, but the importance of the verse has nothing to do with the number of words in it. The important question is, 'Why did Jesus weep?' The obvious answer would be that Jesus came to the home where Lazarus had recently died and when he saw Mary and other friends weeping, he was deeply moved in sympathy and love and he wept with them. It would have been a most natural thing to do, but I do not believe that this is the sole answer. There is clearly more than an element of sympathy in the tears of Jesus, but the context goes way beyond that.

In verse 4 Jesus said that Lazarus' sickness would not end in death. He did not mean that Lazarus would not die, but that the permanent result of that particular illness would not be death. In other words, Jesus fully intended to raise this man from the dead. The delay of two days in responding to the message of Mary and Martha was clearly deliberate. Jesus could have gone immediately and prevented Lazarus from dying, or as he did on another occasion (John 4:50), he could merely have spoken the word and healed the sick brother. He did neither, but waited two days until Lazarus was dead. There is no doubt that this caused the sisters intense anguish and sorrow which Jesus could have prevented but did not. As we have seen, the pain of the few was permitted for the benefit of the whole church in every generation. How much richer are we as Christians because of the incident of the raising of Lazarus! God sometimes allows suffering and pain in order to teach us and others. It is not because he does not love us, but because he loves us so deeply. His delay in flying to our aid may cause momentary anguish but the end result is eternal glory. John Calvin said, 'Let believers learn to suspend their desires if God does not stretch out his hand to help as soon as they think necessity requires. Whatever may be his delays, he never sleeps and never forgets his people.'

It is because of all this that we must conclude that there was much more than just sympathy in the tears of Jesus. So then, what caused the tears? There are three occasions in the Gospels when Jesus wept.

He wept over Jerusalem (Luke 19:41).
He wept in Gethsemane (Matt. 26:39; Luke 22:45; see Heb. 5:7).
He wept in Bethany (John 11:35).

In each case he was weeping over the devastating effects of sin and death. He saw the judgement that would soon fall upon Jerusalem. He felt in Gethsemane the terribleness of the cup of divine wrath that sin had incurred. Here in John 11 we are told twice, in verses 33 and 38, that Jesus was deeply moved in spirit and troubled. D. A. Carson points out that the crucial word here, which the NIV translates as 'deeply moved', 'invariably suggests anger, outrage or emotional indignation'. The word is only used on three other occasions in the New Testament and is translated as follows:

'Warned them sternly' (Matt. 9:30).
'A strong warning' (Mark 1:43).
'Rebuked harshly' (Mark 14:15).

For these reasons Carson translates verses 33 and 38, 'He was outraged in spirit and troubled.'

The tears could not be the normal sorrow of the losing of a loved one, as were the tears of Mary and Martha, because Jesus knew that Lazarus would be alive again in a few minutes. If Carson is right, and as well as sympathy there is also anger in the tears of Jesus, what then was the cause of his anger? Carson answers, 'Some think that Jesus is moved by their grief, and is consequently angry with the sin, sickness and death in this fallen world that wreaks so much havoc and generates so much sorrow. Others think that the anger is directed at the unbelief itself. The men and women before him were grieving like pagans, like "the rest of men, who have no hope" (1 Thess. 4:13). Profound grief at such bereavement is natural enough; grief that degenerates to despair, that pours out its loss as if there were no resurrection, is an implicit denial of that resurrection. Perhaps these two interpretations are not irreconcilable.'

Anger at the devastation sin causes

God hates sin and Jesus weeps over the horror and vileness of sin that destroys man, who is made in the image of God. Death was no part of God's plan for man. Man was created to live, and not to die. Death is the inevitable consequence of sin because sin is a cause of revulsion to God and he will not have it near him. On the first occasion that God was confronted with human sin in Genesis 3, he acted firmly and severely but justly, and the sinners were banished from his holy presence (Gen. 3:24). In Genesis 4 we see sin erupting in violence and death as brother kills brother. By the time of Genesis 6 sin has spread its influence to all the sons and daughters of Adam, and we read in verse 5, 'The Lord saw how great man's wickedness on the earth had become, and that every inclination of the thoughts of his heart was only evil all the time.' Now notice God's reaction in verses 6 and 7: 'The Lord was grieved that he had made man on the earth, and his heart was filled with pain. So the Lord said, "I will wipe mankind, whom I have created, from the face of the earth."'

God treats sin very seriously and nowhere in Scripture does he condone it, or regard it lightly, or dismiss it as irrelevant. This is in distinct contrast to man's attitude both in Scripture and today. In the Old Testament, King Ahab thought it a light thing to sin. He trifled with the law of God and manipulated it to suit himself. Urged on by his wife Jezebel, he spurned the truth of God. The result was misery for many as God dealt with him and the nation. The lesson is that sin cannot be played with.

The same is true today throughout society. Sin is admired,

applauded, made the subject of entertainment, but rarely wept over. Sin has become respectable and acceptable. Then it erupts in riots on the streets and older folk throw up their hands in horror and say the young need more discipline. Sin laughs at this because there is no discipline in the lives of the older people, whether they be politicians or parents. For generations we have courted sin and now we have to live with its offspring of riot, violence, immorality and ungodliness. But still it is applauded and admired and not taken seriously. God takes it seriously. It grieves him and he weeps over it.

In the context of suffering and death this is very important because it answers the questions we all ask at some time or other. Why does God allow terrible diseases, like cancer, to exist? Why does God not do something about it? The cause of all suffering and death in the world is sin. We need to stress again that this does not mean that each particular illness is because of some hidden sin in the sufferer's life. Job's comforters made that mistake. The answer of Jesus to this confused thinking is to be found in Luke 13:1-5.

God is angry with sin and he has done something about it. He sent his Son into the world to bear our sin and guilt, to atone for our violation of the law of God and to free us from the ultimate consequence of sin. This does not mean that the Christian is untroubled by suffering and death. As we have seen in John 11, this Christian family were not spared the ravages of sickness and death, but there is a strength which faith in Christ supplies, and there are a vision and hope that take the Christian past despair and open to him the glories of the one who is the resurrection and the life.

Anger at unbelief

As believers in Christ we have something that ought to remove despair from the death of a loved one. Weep, yes, but do not despair. To do so is to grieve as the world, which sees death as the end, with nothing beyond it. Matthew Henry said of the way Jesus dealt with the sorrowing sisters, 'He would thus divert the grief of his mourning friends, by raising their expectations of something great; as if he had said, "I did not come hither with an address of condolence, to mingle a few fruitless insignificant tears with yours; no, I have other work to do; come, let us adjourn to the grave, and go about our business there."'

Does not our Saviour have the right to be angry when we Christians forget the victory of the cross and the glories of the empty tomb? Would he have to come into our family homes at a time of death and say, 'Why all this commotion and wailing' (Mark 5:39). To quote Matthew Henry again, 'Does this become those who believe in a God, a heaven, and another world?' This is a delicate subject because we all feel sorrow to a different degree and the emotions of some Christians are more demonstrative than others, but none of us must allow deep sorrow to accuse God or to doubt his love and care for us. His love never wavers, even when our doubts and unbelief grieve him so much.

There are two observations made in verses 36 and 37 with regard to the attitude of Jesus towards Lazarus. As far as we are able to see, they were not made by believers, but one is still a simple statement of truth. Jesus loved Lazarus greatly, even as he loves all his people. The other is a carping criticism that should never be found on the lips of a Christian.

Chapter 8

God is in control

The family in Bethany, like most Christian families in a time of sorrow, went through a whole medley of emotions. Add to this the emotion of their friends, and the picture emerges of how ill-equipped most folk are to deal with the death of a loved one. But when the doubts, cynicism and frustration of men and women have had their say, the outstanding fact that remains is the love and power of the Lord Jesus Christ. He knew exactly what he planned to do, and he did it.

In every situation that affects his people the same authority and control are present. The psalmist knew this and was ever delighting in it:

'I sought the Lord, and he answered me;
    he delivered me from all my fears.
Those who look to him are radiant;
    their faces are never covered with shame.

This poor man called, and the Lord heard him;
    he saved him out of all his troubles.
The angel of the Lord encamps around those who fear
    him,
    and he delivers them'

(Ps. 34:4-7).

The apostle Paul, writing from a prison cell in Rome, expresses the same confidence: 'Now I want you to know, brothers, that what has happened to me has really served to advance the gospel. As a result, it has become clear throughout the whole palace guard and to everyone else that I am in chains for Christ. Because of my chains, most of the brothers in the Lord have been encouraged to speak the word of God more courageously and fearlessly' (Phil. 1:12-14).

What an encouragement it is for every Christian to know that God is in control! If we truly believed this we would save ourselves much despair and fear. It is this knowledge that brings peace into suffering and takes the despair out of death. We can learn from this story in John 11 that, though there will be times when events and circumstances may suggest that God has lost control, it is not so. He may allow things to happen that we would rather avoid, and he may take us through paths we would rather not walk, but the end result will always be the glory of God and the strengthening of our faith.

If we have to face situations that may cause us to doubt God's control, our doubts always serve only to increase our pain. When you cannot see clearly or understand what is happening, then as Christians you must walk by faith. In such situations make the words of William Hiley Bathurst your prayer:

Oh, for a faith that will not shrink,
Though pressed by many a foe;
That will not tremble on the brink
Of poverty or woe;

That will not murmur or complain
Beneath the chastening rod;
But in the hour of grief or pain
Can lean upon its God;

A faith that shines more bright and clear
When tempests rage without;
That when in danger knows no fear,
In darkness feels no doubt;

A faith that keeps the narrow way
Till life's last spark is fled,
And with a pure and heavenly ray
Lights up the dying bed!

Lord, give me such a faith as this,
And then, whate'er may come,
I taste e'en now the hallowed bliss
Of an eternal home.

Out of control

As far as Mary and Martha were concerned, Jesus had let the situation go too far. Lazarus was dead and there was no answer to death. This thinking was still dominant even when Jesus told them to roll away the stone from the tomb. Martha immediately objects, 'But, Lord, by this time there is a bad odour, for he has been there four days.' Martha's problem was that the sorrow had caused her to forget so much. She forgot that Jesus had said the sickness would not end in death. She forgot that Jesus had promised, 'Your brother will rise again.' She forgot her own declaration: 'I believe that you are the Christ, the Son of God.' And perhaps even more surprisingly, she forgot her own confidence in verse 22: 'Even now God will give you whatever you ask.' She forgot, and in her despair she says, in effect, 'There is no point in rolling away the stone. It is too late. It is hopeless. There is nothing Jesus can do.' The result is that she stands in the way and seeks to prevent the very thing she wants above all else.

Most of us have been in a similar situation. There is much unbelief still in our hearts. It is easy to talk of faith in days of health and prosperity, but much harder to practise it in days of adversity.

Jesus deals with this battered and bewildered saint in a most tender way. Verse 40 is a rebuke: 'Did I not tell you that if you believed, you would see the glory of God?' It is a rebuke, but oh, how gentle! There is much we can learn in dealing with each other from how Jesus dealt with Martha. Sorrow puts faith under intense pressure. Christians in this position do not need harsh criticism or empty platitudes, but gentle rebuke in reminding them again of the promises and goodness of God.

Resurrection

Lazarus was dead; of that there was no doubt. Jesus, with many hostile witnesses looking on, raised this man from the dead. There is no doubt of that either, for in the next chapter we find Lazarus having dinner with friends and also the priests plotting to kill him and so, as they saw it, destroy the proof of Christ's amazing power. Lazarus was alive. God was glorified. Jesus was demonstrated to be in total control of life and death. This Christian family was reunited and joy displaced sorrow.

What help is this to us when we lose a loved one to death? We do not expect to see someone we buried walking around a week later, so is there any relevance in this for us? Firstly, let us acknowledge that this really happened. This is not a fairy story! Also we should acknowledge that there must have been many corpses lying in graves in Bethany, but Jesus only raised one from the dead. Lazarus was raised, as Jesus said in verse 42, that people might believe that God sent his Son into this world. The encouragement for us is the gospel truth that God sent Jesus to us — to die in our place and purchase for us life instead of death. The whole message of the gospel tells us that what Jesus did for Lazarus, he is going to do for every dead Christian. A Christian is someone who by the grace of God has been saved from the consequence of sin. He has passed from death to life. His soul is saved and, while it is true that his body will die and go to the grave, that will not be the end. In John 5:25-29 Jesus tells us, 'I tell you the truth, a time is coming and has now come when the dead will hear the voice of the Son of God and those who hear will live. For as the Father has life in himself, so he has granted the Son to have life in himself. And he has given him authority to judge because he is the Son of Man. Do not be amazed at this, for a time is coming when all who are in their graves will hear his voice and come out — those who have done good will rise to live, and those who have done evil will rise to be condemned.'

God has fixed a day when what happened to Lazarus will happen to all dead believers, but with a glorious difference. Lazarus was raised to live again in a body of sin and in a world of sin. Consequently one day he would have to go back to the grave. On that great Day of the Lord we and Lazarus will all be raised with new bodies, which are like Christ's glorious body, and we shall live in a new heaven and a new earth where there will be no sin at all and no more dying.

That is the hope of the gospel, so when we bury Christians we do so with this wonderful prospect in mind. As we stand at their graves and weep for our loss, we can also rejoice that one day Jesus will stand at that grave, and the graves will give up their dead in obedience to the sovereign voice of God. No wonder Paul said that we are to encourage each other with this truth! This is not 'pie in the sky when you die' but the achievement of the love and power of our God and Saviour.

Sickness _and_ Death

IN THE CHRISTIAN FAMILY

The resurrection of the body

The doctrine of the resurrection of the Lord Jesus Christ from the dead is the heart of biblical Christianity. It was the centre and emphasis of all the apostolic preaching from Pentecost onwards. The apostles did what we would regard as misguided — they put all their eggs in one basket. They stood or fell by the doctrine of the resurrection. It was a truth that on occasions got them into trouble. In Acts 17, when Paul preached at Athens to the learned philosophers, out of intellectual curiosity they listened to him, but when he mentioned the resurrection they sneered. The same thing is found in Acts 25:19. Paul was imprisoned because of 'a dead man named Jesus whom Paul claimed was alive'.

If this doctrine was so controversial, why did they not play it down and refrain from giving it such prominence? The answer is that they were men under orders. Their business was to preach the gospel, and the resurrection of

Christ is the heart of this message. Paul stresses this in 1 Corinthians 15:17: 'If Christ has not been raised, your faith is futile; you are still in your sins.'

The apostles' doctrine of resurrection did not stop with Christ being raised from the dead. They also taught the resurrection of all believers, that is, the bodily resurrection of all Christians from the grave to share in the eternal life of Christ in heaven. Our souls have been redeemed but there is also to be a redemption of the body when the Lord comes a second time (Rom. 8:23); that is why Paul is able to say in 1 Corinthians 15:19, 'If only for this life we have hope in Christ, we are to be pitied more than all men.' There is a future life in Christ and that involves the body as well as the spirit.

Firstfruits

In 1 Corinthians 15, after establishing the fact of the bodily resurrection of Christ, from verse 20 to the end of the chapter Paul deals with the bodily resurrection of all Christians. The case is detailed and closely argued but thrilling. It appears that there were some in the Corinthian church who, while they believed in Christ's resurrection, did not believe in the resurrection of all believers. Paul states in verse 20 that Christ was raised as the firstfruits of all Christians. The firstfruits in the Old Testament were the first sheaf of harvest that was brought as an offering to God. This was a guarantee or assurance of the ingathering of the whole harvest. This was only one sheaf but there were thousands to follow. So Christ's resurrection is a guarantee of the resurrection of all his people. He is risen as the firstfruits, or in his own words, 'Because I live, you also will live.'

What kind of body?

Those who did not believe in the resurrection of Christians were asking two questions: 'How are the dead raised?' and, 'With what kind of body will they come?' It seems from Paul's answer in 1 Corinthians 15:36, 'How foolish!', that these questions were asked to ridicule the concept of resurrection. But they can also be genuine questions in the mind of a confused Christian. He witnesses a loved one being cremated and the body totally destroyed. Or another Christian may be blown to pieces in an explosion, or even if someone is buried all that is left after a time is bones. So what sort of bodies will these people have in a resurrection?

Such thinking fails to take into consideration the life-giving power of God all around us in nature. It is no problem to God, if he so wishes, to bring the atoms that make up a body from a million places in the earth, and form them together again. Cremation, explosion, drowning or burial make no difference to the resurrection. Paul illustrates this from verse 37 onwards by calling upon us to consider an ordinary thing like a seed. Matthew Henry comments, 'It is a foolish thing to question the divine power to raise the dead when we see it every day in reviving things that are dead.'

The illustration is very simple and is similar to the one Jesus used in John 12:24: 'Unless a grain of wheat falls to the ground and dies, it remains only a single seed. But if it dies, it produces many seeds.' When you buy a packet of seeds for your garden they do not look very much. They are small, dead-looking, and totally unattractive, but from them will come beautiful flowers. You look at the small seed and you can only explain the miracle of growth to full harvest if you put God behind it and say, as Paul does in verse 38, 'God gives it a body.' We can appreciate this in terms of a seed, but verse 42 goes on, 'So will it be with the resurrection of the dead.'

It needs to be stressed that in 1 Corinthians 15 the apostle is dealing with the *bodily* resurrection of Christians and not with spiritual resurrection. So when the question is asked, 'What kind of body?' the answer is a new body. Twice, in verses 51 and 52, we are told we shall be changed. It is a changed body. Notice how Paul describes the change. He talks of the dead body of the Christian being sown: not buried, but sown. When you bury something, that is the end of it; but when you sow something you are expecting a future. Death is not the end, but only a stage on the journey to heaven. The body is sown in order to be raised.

The changed body

There are four ways in which the resurrected body will be different from the one we have now (1 Cor. 15:42-44).

1. It is sown perishable, but it is raised imperishable

The moment we are born, the process of perishing, decay and ageing begins and will continue to the grave. The body is full of aches and pain and decay. It is dying all the time, but the resurrected body is different. It is incapable of decay. It has not a blemish, not a fault, not a wrinkle, but is characterized by an eternal freshness.

2. It is sown in dishonour, it is raised in glory

Dishonour means that when the body dies it loses what Charles Hodge calls its 'short-lived attractiveness which it had while living'. That attractiveness is cut off, whether in its teens, middle age or old age. It is cut off and it goes to the grave in dishonour, but it is raised in glory. It will be raised so that our lowly bodies will be like the glorious body of the Lord Jesus Christ (Phil. 3:31) That is a truth to ponder and praise God for.

3. *It is sown in weakness, it is raised in power*

As Charles Hodge says, 'Nothing is more absolutely power-less than a corpse — it can do nothing, and it can resist nothing. The weakness which belonged to it in life is perfected in death.'

The strongest man, like the weakest, is very vulnerable. The same bullet or the same germ can snuff out his life as easily as that of a comparatively weak man. Death strikes where it wills—the weak or the strong, the young or the old. Death brings us all to the same condition, but the Christian is raised in power. The new body will vibrate with energy and vitality — no walking sticks, no hearing aids or spec-tacles! We shall not need them because we shall have legs that never grow weak, ears that never fail and eyes that never grow dim.

4. *It is sown a natural body, it is raised a spiritual body*

The natural body always knows the pull of sin; therefore it has to be mastered and kept in subjection. Paul longed to be delivered from this body of death (Rom. 7:24). The resur-rected body is spiritual and is no longer subject to the pull of sin but is under the complete control of the Holy Spirit.

Rejoice

There is only one possible reaction to all this, and that is to rejoice in wonder and awe at what God is promising us. As you read 1 Corinthians 15, you can feel the excitement building up. You feel the joy growing until Paul reaches that great crescendo of praise at the end of the chapter: '"Death has been swallowed up in victory."

"Where, O death, is your victory?
Where, O death, is your sting?"

'The sting of death is sin, and the power of sin is the law. But thanks be to God! He gives us the victory through our Lord Jesus Christ.'

Every Christian has a glorious future. Death is not the end: it is only a sowing to be followed by the resurrection. This is what the gospel has accomplished for us. Christ has gained the victory over death and the grave, and he has gained it for us. Our problem very often is that we are too earthbound. We need to lift our gaze to the eternal reality of what Christ has done for us. Then we shall be able to stand firm and not be moved by circumstances, or be depressed by a sense of hopelessness, because we know that our labour in the Lord is not in vain.

Sickness *and* Death

IN THE CHRISTIAN FAMILY

Chapter 10

The Christian under stress

Prolonged illness or bereavement inevitably bring pressures upon the Christian. In this area of life the Christian is no different from the non-Christian. The difference will be in how the Christian copes with the stress of illness and death.

In Psalm 62 we find David under great stress. What has caused it we do not know. Some think this psalm was written at the time of his son Absalom's rebellion against him. David was put off the throne by his son and we can imagine the stress that would cause him. Whether this is the background to the psalm or not does not matter; what is important is how David coped with the stress.

In verses 3 and 4 David describes something of the problem he is facing. This is causing him very real difficulties, but there is no depression or fear. Here is great encouragement for us. Stress and fear do not have to go together.

Sadly, so often one leads to the other, but there is no necessity for this if you are a Christian. How can we avoid fear and depression while under stress?

Speaking to ourselves

We need to learn to speak to ourselves about God, to tell our souls to find rest in God alone. It is said that when a man talks to himself it is the first sign of madness. I do not know how true that is, but I do know that when a Christian can talk to himself about God it is a sure sign of spiritual health. In verse 5 David tells his soul to find rest in God alone. He reminds himself that God is his rock and salvation and his fortress, and because this is true, then in spite of the pressures, he will not be shaken. He is reminding himself who God is and what God has done for him.

This is important, because all too often stress tends to produce an introverted self-pity which sees no hope. There are very few things more damaging for a Christian than self-pity. The remedy for this is to see God in all his glory, which will produce in us a most reasonable optimism. No believer can wallow in self-pity when he is aware that his hope comes from God. The magnificence and benevolence of God are our hope and strength, and when we dwell on these truths, even though the problems do not go away we begin to see them in perspective. If you just dwell on the problem and forget God, then you will see no answer, no hope, and you are left with depression.

The Christian does not believe in bypassing problems. We do not whistle in the dark and pretend the difficulties are not there. That is foolishness. That is what tranquillizers and alcohol do. They make you feel at peace, but the problem has not been faced or dealt with. Whatever is causing us difficulties, whether it be illness, death or anything else, these things are real and have to be faced. But face them in the context of the greatness of the God who loves you. This we do by learning to talk to ourselves about God.

Surely this is part of what the Bible calls meditation. It is to be still and remind ourselves of God. The hymn-book is a wonderful help in this. Just turn over the pages and read the hymns, and you will be reminded of the greatness of God. A good hymn-book is one that is full of the goodness and magnificence of God. The great hymns always show you God, and your heart is warmed and encouraged. This helps you and then you will be able to help others in need. In Psalm 62 David spends seven verses delighting in God; only then in verse 8 does he encourage others to do the same.

This is something very practical. Have you ever tried to encourage some other Christian who is going through a rough time? Your motive is right and you say all the right things but you know as you speak that you are not helping him. Why not? Is it not because all you are giving him is words, and he needs more than words? To really be a help we need to come to such people from the presence of God, with our minds and hearts, as well as our words, full of the greatness of God. Talk to yourself first about God; then when you talk to others something of the very fragrance of God will be conveyed to them.

Knowing ourselves

David was a great man, with many God-given gifts, but under pressure he saw himself as a 'leaning wall' and a 'tottering fence'. What a vivid description this is! Have you ever seen a leaning wall? The foundations are insecure, frost has got into the cement and the whole thing is in a state of collapse. One little push and it would be over. The tottering fence is the same. The wooden posts in the ground have rotted. Neglect and wear have taken their toil and it looks as if a strong wind would bring it down. That is how David saw himself in his problems — no stability, no permanence, no strength, nothing to admire, all so frail and on the verge of collapse. He was beginning to see that all that men put their trust in, position and wealth (vv. 9-10), count for nothing in the end.

Such a view would drive most men to despair. But not the Christian, because his rest and hope and strength are not found in himself, but in God alone.

Theory or reality

No true Christian would dispute this. We find this is the teaching of Scripture and we accept it, but is it just theory to us, or is it a reality? The answer to this will depend on whether or not our priorities are correct. Jesus asked, 'What good will it be for a man if he gains the whole world, yet forfeits his soul?' The soul of man must be our first priority and David, in spite of the precarious position in which he found himself, was able to be at peace because his soul had found rest in God.

What is the soul? It is not an easy word to define and Christians disagree over its precise meaning, but for our purposes I will define the soul as that which distinguishes man from all other created beings, and it is immortal. When God breathed into Adam he became a living soul. It is our souls that give us our worth; therefore when Jesus said, 'Do not be afraid of those who kill the body but cannot kill the soul. Rather, be afraid of the One who can destroy both soul and body in hell,' he was emphasizing the supreme value and priority of the soul. Jesus never taught that the body was unimportant. On the contrary, he cared for people's bodies, he healed them and fed them, but the soul takes top priority.

We need to learn this, and sometimes it is only acute stress that reveals whether or not we really do believe it. Let me give you an example. In August 1985 I was preaching at an open-air service on the promenade in Aberystwyth. I stressed to the listening crowd the importance and consequence of knowing God. I said the Christian was sure to go to heaven because of the salvation he had in Christ. I said if I was to die tonight I knew I would go to heaven. I believed this and preached it passionately, but ten minutes after preaching I had a heart attack and finished up in hospital. As I lay there all the words that I had been preaching with such passion and enthusiasm began to challenge me. Did I really believe them? The heart attack had suddenly brought the whole issue of life and death into clearer focus. I was now faced with the reality of all that I thought I believed. How do we Christians cope in such situations?

David said, 'My soul finds rest in God alone.' Rest in God, not only in the good times but also in the bad. When the body is racked with pain, when the emotions are bruised and torn in bereavement — even then we can find rest.

Finding rest

Soul rest is not something that comes automatically, because sadly some do not experience it in times of stress. It is a rest that has to be found. You find something in one of two ways: either accidentally or by searching. Often you do not even know that something exists, so consequently you do not look for it, but suddenly, accidentally, you find it. On the other hand, you are aware of something that you do not possess, so you search for it. There can be a lot of frustration and disappointment in searching, but if you are desperate enough you do not give up until you find. Rest of soul is not found accidentally, but by searching. You know it is possible because God has promised it. You know as a Christian you ought to have it and need it, so you search. In other words you look to God. You ask. You pray and you do not give up until you find it. We shall see in the next chapter from Psalm 63 how to find this rest, but for the moment let us ask, 'What is rest of soul?'

Rest of soul

In Psalm 62 David is in trouble and he realizes how weak he is — nothing but a leaning wall and a tottering fence. But he does not stop there. He looks beyond his difficulties to the greatness and goodness of God. Rest of soul is to get things into perspective. It is to realize what we are and what we have in God. We have salvation (v. 1). We have strength because God is our rock (v. 2). We have security because God is our fortress (v. 2) We have stability because we shall never be moved or shaken (v. 2). We have hope (v. 5) and honour (v. 7). All these blessings are to be found in God alone. They can be found nowhere else. They are mercies that do not merely come *from* God; they are only found *in* God. You cannot have them in detachment from God. God is not like a doctor who gives you a prescription and you go away and benefit from the remedy. Rest of soul is found in God, in oneness and fellowship with God. It is dependent upon the union we have with Christ.

This rest is not an emotional feeling. It is certainly not gritting your teeth and bearing it stoically. It is not putting on a brave face in time of trouble. Rest of soul is resting in and embracing and experiencing the beauty and wonder of our God and Saviour. It is enjoying God when you may not be enjoying much else. It is not something theoretical, but a deep reality of the peace and love and sufficiency of God. It is rest in him.

When I was in hospital with the heart attack in 1985, for a few days I did not want to do anything, but then I picked up a book I had been reading. It was Eifion Evans' biography of Daniel Rowlands, and before being taken ill I had read up to page 300. In hospital I resumed my reading and on page 302 I came across a hymn by William Williams that I had never seen before. Apart from Scripture no words ever spoke to me so powerfully as these:

> To see thy face, Beloved, makes my poor soul rejoice,
> O'er all I've ever tasted, or ever made my choice;
> When they all disappear, why should I grieve or pine
> While to my gaze there opens the sight that Christ is
>   mine?

> He's greater than his blessing, he's greater than his
>   grace,
> Far greater than his actions, whatever you may trace;
> I'll plead for faith, gifts, cleansing; for these I'll yearn
>   quite sore,
> But on him only, always, I'll look and lean far more.

I felt so weak and helpless, and did not know if I would ever be able to preach again. The things I enjoyed and valued most looked like ending. But, said Williams, 'When they all disappear why should I grieve or pine, while to my gaze there opens the sight that Christ is mine?' Nothing changes our relationship to the Lord Jesus Christ. If everything else goes, his love still shines through. What rest of soul that great truth brought to me! Jesus is greater than his blessings, his grace or his actions. It is perfectly legitimate to plead for faith, gifts and cleansing, but the supreme thing for the Christian is to look and lean far more on the Saviour.

Rest of soul is to know what it is to look and lean when all other things fall apart. This is what David is saying in Psalm 62. In the silence and loneliness of pain and sorrow Christ remains our sufficiency. This is the glorious reality of the Christian faith: feeling the pain and sorrow but still being at rest.

Sickness *and* Death
IN THE CHRISTIAN FAMILY

Chapter 11

Finding rest

In the previous chapter we saw from Psalm 62 that the Christian under great stress can know rest of soul, but this does not come automatically. It has to be found. In Psalm 63 David tells us how to find it. In the midst of problems and pressures we are not to sit around and mope with a vague hope that things will get better: we are to seek earnestly.

It is easier to say this than to do it, and while all believers in times of comfort will acknowledge that this is the correct thing to do, when the stress comes we seem to get confused and uncertain. David was aware of this and he realized that we need an incentive to seek God. This man of God is not theorizing but facing real problems. Charles Spurgeon wrote, 'This was probably written while David was fleeing from Absalom; certainly at the time he wrote it he was king (v. 11), and hard pressed by those who sought his life. David did not leave off singing because he was in the wilderness, neither did he in slovenly idleness go on repeating Psalms intended for other occasions; but he carefully made his worship suitable to his circumstances, and presented to his God a wilderness hymn when he was in the wilderness. There was no desert in his heart, though there was a desert around him. We too may expect to be cast into rough places ere we go hence. In such seasons, may the Eternal Comforter abide with us, and cause us to bless the Lord at all times, making even the solitary places to become a temple for Jehovah.'

If we are to know the Eternal Comforter with us then we need to listen to David's advice. The incentive he had to seek God is expressed in Psalm 63:2,3: 'I have seen you in the sanctuary and beheld your power and glory,' and because of this the psalmist could say, 'Your love is better than life.'

Our incentive to seek God

The incentive to seek God is that we are clear in our minds as to who God is and what he is to his people. In other words, the incentive to seek is that you know there is someone and something to be found. If a man goes prospecting for gold it is because, rightly or wrongly, he believes there is gold to be found. His seeking is prompted by his believing.

We may come into situations, caused by illness, bereavement or something else, and begin to think there is no answer. But because we are Christians we know there is an answer. We may not have it at the moment, but we know it is to be found. The answer is God and, whatever problem we have to face, we can always say like David, 'O God, you are my God.' Nothing changes that. If this is true, why is it that we have to seek God? The answer is because the problems so often overwhelm us and we lose sight of God. He is still there, but we allow the problems to block him out. Our *doctrine* may still be perfectly all right but our *experience* of God has gone haywire. We succumb to the pressures and our view of God is lost, or at best confused.

In such situations we do as David did. We must draw on past experiences. That is what verse 2 is about. There was no sanctuary in the desert of Judah, but that did not prevent David from remembering past blessings and experiences of God. I am not encouraging us to live in the past. You cannot live on past blessings, but you can use them as an incentive to seek God and know those blessings again. This is what David is doing. When there is darkness in the soul and you can find no help from Scripture or worship or fellowship, and those things that were once a blessing to you, you now avoid — we can all know periods like this — then your only hope is to remember better days and richer experiences of God. Remember the times when prayer was a joy and fellowship a delight, when the Word spoke so clearly and so often to you. Your hope is that God is unchanging and what you knew once you can know again.

How to seek God

We are to seek earnestly, and there are two reasons for this. The first is the character of God, and the second is the desperate need we have. The picture painted in this psalm is very vivid. When a man is lost in a desert there is only one thing he wants. You can offer him wealth, fame, position or promotion, but he is not interested. These things are of no more value to him than the sand under his feet. The only thing he wants is water. His whole life is reduced to one basic requirement — water.

Similarly, a Christian under stress, that has perhaps led him into a spiritual desert, says with David,

'My soul thirsts for you,
    my body longs for you,
in a dry and weary land
    where there is no water.'

That is earnest seeking. This man is not playing at Christianity. Every atom and fibre of his being long for God. Nothing else will satisfy him. He will not be satisfied with a little blessing from God; he wants God himself. This man is now taken up with God more than his problems. In verse 6 he tells us that he cannot get God out of his mind. He cannot sleep because he is thinking about God. Our problem so often is that we cannot sleep because we are worrying about our difficulties. Remember David is not writing this during a period of ease and comfort, but in a time of acute difficulties, and his problems have not gone away. He tells us in verses 9 and 10 that his enemies are still active, but he is not worried about them because he knows he is in God's hands and God will deal with them.

At this point rest of soul is beginning to make itself known to David. Peace is drawing near. The problem is still real, but God is more real. Rest of soul is not some magical experience; it is simply seeking God before all things. When God is in the centre of the Christian's focus, even though the problems still have to be dealt with, then there is rest and peace. This is not some glib, easy remedy; it is getting to grips with God. In Psalm 62:8 David describes it as pouring out your heart to him. This will involve not only bringing our fears and sorrows to God, but also our sin and disobedience. Very often the greatest stress caused to the Christian is an unwillingness to go God's way. On many occasions our difficulties are caused not originally by our *actions,* but by our *reactions* to people and situations. We may be suffering unjustly, but the way we cope with that may be sinful. Pour out your heart to God, says David, and trust him at all times. Then, and only then, will we stay close to God and know that the divine hand upholds (Ps. 63:8).

The Christian finds rest of soul when he is acutely aware of his own weakness and of the infinite greatness and goodness of God. In God alone is rest, and the result in Psalm 63 is praise (v. 4), satisfaction (v. 5), joy (v. 11) and a determination (v. 8) to stay close to God and not lose again the sense of the presence and peace of God. Our hope is the character of God, and in times of great difficulties our hope for deliverance is not in the pastor, or the church, or Christian friends (though we thank God for these), but our hope is in God alone. So we are to seek him earnestly, and we do so in the knowledge that he is already seeking us. Seek and you will find.

Sickness _and_ Death

IN THE CHRISTIAN FAMILY

Chapter 12

A personal experience

I include this last chapter in the hope that my own experience of sickness and death might help the reader.

My first experience of death was at the age of fifteen, when my father died. I will never forget that Friday in October 1952. It was the most happy and the most sad day of my life up to that point. My father was keen on sport and always encouraged me to play. So when that day in school I was told I had been picked to play rugby for Neath schoolboys the next day against Cardiff, I was overjoyed. I was given the famous Neath black jersey and could not get home quick enough to show my father. He was ill in bed, and I had no idea how ill he was, but by the time I arrived home he was dead. Shock, anger and numbness were emotions that seemed to explode in my mind all at the same time. I was not a Christian and had no God to turn to. Death was so cruel, pointless and final.

I became a Christian in 1955 and was married in 1958. Death next touched me the following year when my daughter died. She was born with spina bifida and only lived for nine days. My wife and I were heartbroken but we had a God to turn to. In a most remarkable way through that dark experience the Lord spoke quite independently to both of us and the result was my call into the Christian ministry. I had been preaching since I was eighteen and had no desire at all to leave a good job in industry and enter the ministry. Now the call was very clear. About a year later, on the day I was accepted for training in the theological college, we knew that another baby was on the way. God's ways are mysterious but he is gentle, loving and tender in all his dealings with his people.

I had always enjoyed good health and had never been in hospital until 1984. From 1984 until the time of writing this, all that has changed. Ill-health and hospitals seem to dominate my life. Two operations in 1984 and a heart attack in 1985 changed everything. I was determined that these things were not going to hinder my ministry and six months after the heart attack I was on a two-month preaching tour of Australia where I preached fifty-five times in fifty-six days. All seemed well again until November 1987 when I suddenly began to be very tired. It seems as if several times a week all my energy, from head to foot, drained away. It was diagnosed as Myalgic Encephalomyelitis, commonly known as ME. This is a very disabling illness and I could not think straight, my concentration span was only about thirty minutes and my memory was affected. During this period only the grace of God enabled me to preach and preparation was almost non-existent. This lasted for nearly four years and when at last the effects of ME started to wane, angina flared up. In April 1991 suddenly it was difficult to walk a hundred yards because of the angina. I was sent for an angiogram and as a result of this the cardiologist told me that I had a serious heart condition and needed a triple bypass operation. I wrote much of this book while waiting to go into hospital for the operation.

What have these experiences taught me? Unquestionably they have enriched my spiritual life. Do not misunderstand me. I am not recommending these things as a means to blessing. But the fact is that in them God has drawn near. The experiences of losing my father while only a teenager and then losing a baby daughter have enabled me to understand and sympathize with, and minister to, those who have gone through similar sorrows, in a way that would not have been possible otherwise. In health or sickness, joy or sorrow, God is still the same loving, heavenly Father.

The eight years from 1984 to 1991 were, healthwise, very difficult and at times frustrating as I was unable to work with the energy and drive of previous years. But they were not wasted or unprofitable years. We all have to work for God within the limits set upon us by health or ability or circumstances. Whatever the limitations, we are still to work with all our heart. We are not to use poor health or anything else we may not have as an excuse for disobedience. We cannot control our limitations, but we can control the effort and enthusiasm we put into our Christian life. Give your best and God will give the grace to use it to his praise and glory.

He giveth more grace when the burdens grow greater,
He sendeth more strength when the labours increase;
To added affliction he addeth his mercy,
To multiplied trials, his multiplied peace.

When we have exhausted our store of endurance,
When our strength has failed ere the day is half done,
When we reach the end of our hoarded resources,
Our Father's full giving is only begun.

His love has no limit, his grace has no measure,
His power has no boundary known unto men;
For out of his infinite riches in Jesus
He giveth, and giveth, and giveth again!

(Annie Johnson Flint).

Bibliography

Quotations have been taken from the following sources:

Boettner, L. *Immortality,* Presbyterian and Reformed.
Carson, D. A. *The Gospel of John,* IVP.
Hendriksen, W. *John,* Banner of Truth.
Henry, Matthew. *Commentary,* Wm Mackenzie.
M'Cheyne, Robert Murray. *Comfort in sickness and sorrow,* Baker.
Murray, I. *The fight of faith,* Banner of Truth.
Pink, A. W. *The Gospel of John,* Zondervan.
Ryle, J. C. *Expository Thoughts on the Gospels,* James Clark.e.
Ryle, J. C. *Sickness,* Evangelical Press.
Spurgeon, C. H. *The Treasury of David,* Marshall, Morgan & Scott.

GREAT GOD
of
WONDERS

The attributes of God

PETER JEFFERY

Written to help those beginning the Christian life to see something of what God has revealed about himself. Practical application by an author well known for his books that help new Christians.

ISBN 0 85234 302 7